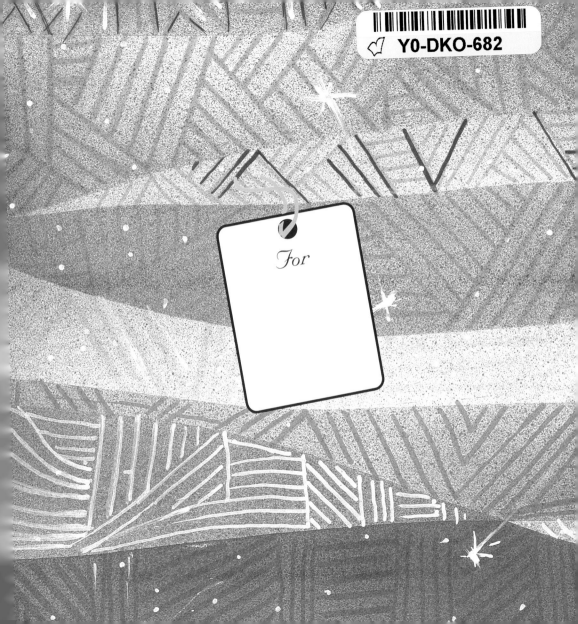

For

A GOSPEL CHRISTMAS

By Sonya Tinsley

Illustrated by Angela Williams
Designed by Lesley Ehlers

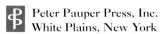 Peter Pauper Press, Inc.
White Plains, New York

Born in a Manger

In many ways, the story of gospel music *is* the story of Christmas. Just as the infant Jesus was born into the meanest of circumstances, only later to be honored and adored the world over, gospel music—once an object of scorn and derision—is now one of the world's most cherished and beloved art forms.

The story of gospel's humble beginnings, like the story of Christ's birth, reminds us that our richest treasures can arise from the poorest of origins. Jesus was born in a manger. The seeds of gospel were conceived in the cotton fields and backwoods houses of the South, and gospel sprang forth from the

tenements and storefront churches of the North. Jesus' earthly parents were outcasts. Gospel was birthed out of the experiences of the disenfranchised and disrespected African-American people. To borrow the words of the legendary civil rights organizer Fannie Lou Hamer, African-Americans were a people who had grown "sick and tired of being sick and tired." At the outset, gospel was disdained by some who were afraid of being tainted by the music of those they considered to be their inferiors. Much time and many changes would pass before gospel music would come to be what it is today—an inspiration to people of all races, classes, and nationalities.

It would appear that God appreciates few things more than a jubilant gospel mass choir—complete with drums and tambourines, of course!

O clap your hands, all ye people; shout unto God with the voice of triumph . . . Sing praises to God, sing praises; sing praises unto our King, sing praises.

Psalms 47:1, 6 (KJV)

Make a joyful noise unto the LORD, all the earth: make a loud noise, and rejoice, and sing praise. Sing unto the LORD with the harp, and the voice of a psalm. With trumpets and sound of cornet make a joyful noise before the LORD, the King. Let the sea

roar, and the fulness thereof; the world and they that dwell therein. Let the floods clap their *hands: let the hills be joyful together . . .*

Psalms 98:4-8 (KJV)

Make a joyful noise unto the LORD, *all ye lands. Serve the* LORD *with gladness: come before his presence with singing. . . . Enter into his gates with thanksgiving* and *into his courts with praise: be thankful unto him,* and *bless his name.*

Psalms 100:1-2, 4 (KJV)

GOSPEL IS AS GOSPEL DOES

Gospel music is marked by a particular style of singing and expression. Gwendolin Sims Warren writes, "It is a feeling, or an expression of feelings, that releases its singers to 'sing a new song' even while repeating the already familiar words." In fact, gospel songs are often stylized versions of traditional spirituals and hymns. Both lyrically and melodically, gospel songs borrow freely from one another. True to the spirit of the Gospel itself, the spirit and emotion of the song is often more important than its authorship. This is not to belittle the artistic achievements of the many legendary gospel composers. The

essence of gospel music is in its sincere and impassioned delivery whether the song is a composition of a particular composer or an arrangement of a traditional song. Gospel artists have the ability to transform *any* song into a gospel song. Vocalists reshape the lyrics and melodies of their selections to suit the feelings and needs of the present moment. Standard hymns such as "Amazing Grace," "His Eye Is On the Sparrow," "Blessed Assurance (Jesus Is Mine)," or "Rock of Ages" are transformed from their conventional form once a choir or soloist, working that gospel magic, has imparted a sense of tangible emotion to those of us in the audience. And of course we are expected to join in. There are no sidelines in gospel music!

SPIRITUAL ROOTS

The history of gospel music is entwined with the black experience in America. Although gospel music as a distinct musical genre did not appear until the 1920s, it is a direct descendant of the spirituals created by enslaved African-Americans. In the ever-popular African-American hymnal *Songs of Zion*, J. Jefferson Cleveland and William B. McClain write, "Many of the early gospel songs were simply arrangements and adaptations of spirituals." Adapters such as "Thomas A. Dorsey, Sallie Martin, Roberta Martin, Robert Johnson, Myrtle Jackson, Kenneth Morris, and James Cleveland" brought updated versions of the "Negro spirituals" into the twentieth century. It is not unusual for

contemporary gospel compositions to borrow phrases, sections, and even whole melodies from these African-American religious folk songs.

Spirituals were created by African-Americans collectively and passed around communities and through generations. Spirituals are so named because our enslaved grandparents believed these songs were the voice of the Holy Spirit speaking both to and through the faithful. It is for this reason that no one person was given credit for "composing" a spiritual. Like the Biblical Gospel texts, spirituals were considered by our ancestors to be the Word of the Lord revealing itself to humanity. As spirituals traveled, new lines were added and old lines were taken away in whatever manner the Holy Spirit seemed to dictate. This spirit of improvisation and spontaneity is still predominant in the gospel music we enjoy today.

Spirituals are often mistakenly typecast as sorrow songs. Many

spirituals could accurately be portrayed as such, but just as often these songs are anything but downcast. Gospel music owes much of its joy and energy to the African oral tradition of call and response, which is the format of many spirituals. Rather than listening quietly to one person sing, the heirs of African culture in the New World have preferred singing to be a communal experience. In this tradition, the line between audience and performer is almost completely eliminated. The clapping and musical response of all of us in the room is just as integral to the song as the soloist's or song leader's part. The *Songs of Zion* hymnal states:

> *Accompanying the singing of the spiritual at all times was some form of body movement—shouting, dancing, hand clapping, foot tapping, foot stamping, or swaying of the body. The singers were bound by no rules; yet chants, hums, wailings, shouts, glides, turns, groans,*

moans, word interjections, and so on were not used indiscriminately, as they might appear, but were used as special devices to urge the singer on to exciting and climactic performances. These practices are typically African.

It is because the spirituals have always belonged to everyone, rather than a few select persons, that their presence is still so vibrant. To the present day, it is not only expected but also encouraged for random members of the group to take turns making up new verses for the rest to follow. This practice of having song leaders call out lines for the community to sing along proved to be an ingenious way for a creative people to share songs and Biblical stories of faith during a time when slavery and illiteracy prevented them from utilizing the written word.

Calling upon Jesus as their help, they plotted and planned for their freedom just as their descendants would do behind the wood and brick walls of visible churches during the Civil Rights Movement. Back out in the fields and inside the kitchens, our ancestors could share both their stories and their strategies by disguising them inside the melody of a sweet-sounding spiritual. They knew just how to sing about going to "glory" so that the right ears could hear and know that they were really talking about going North. Walking around the plantation, they might have pretended to be oblivious to the larger significance of Christmas. However, deep inside the hush harbors they were at precious liberty to sing their own truth, including the story of a Savior born to protect and strengthen them in their secret struggle for freedom.

For the slaves, the holiday season meant three to five days without heavy labor. On some plantations, the length of the holiday break depended on how long the Yule log burned. In such situations, our ancestors took on the Yule log tradition as a challenge to their ingenuity and devised creative ways to ensure that a single log burned longer than anyone could have imagined.

Another holiday tradition was the game of "Christmas Gif'." The point of the game was to surprise others throughout the day by crying out "Christmas gif'" before they had an opportunity to do the same to you. The last person to get the words out was obligated to come up with some small token to give as a present, whether a fistful of nuts, a pretty scrap of fabric, or a handful of tea cakes baked just for this occasion. Part of the fun for many of our ancestors was to be deliberately slow in calling out "Christmas gif'" in order to relish the rare opportunity to present friends and neighbors with gifts. Under the harsh conditions of slavery, having something extra to give away was an infrequent and prized luxury.

How many of us who now have so much to give actually relish the opportunity to do so? How many of us think of giving, itself, as the treat?

Although the joy our ancestors managed to create for themselves during the holidays may seem meager to us who live in contemporary times, it was so much joy to them that they dubbed New Year's Day, the last day of the holiday season, "Heartbreak Day." On Heartbreak Day, families and friends living on different plantations were forced to leave each other again after barely getting used to the idea of being together. After Heartbreak Day, it was back to business as usual on the plantation until the de big time rolled around again.

Today, in thinking about something as painful as Heartbreak Day, it seems wonderful that husbands and wives, sisters and brothers, and parents and children are actually together enough in their present lives to get on each other's nerves. For our ancestors, however, so many of life's pleasures had to be postponed until Christmas of the next year.

THE MANGER OR THE CROSS?

It is curious, as many scholars of African-American religious music have noted, that of all the varied subjects touched upon by our spirituals and gospel songs, those celebrating Christmas are the fewest in number. Perhaps, as suggested by James Weldon Johnson, African-Americans preferred to think of Jesus as God, as almighty and all-powerful, and this idea of Him could not be easily reconciled with His being born of a woman. Jesus in the older Spirituals is generally given a title of power—most often He is called "King Jesus."

This may well be the correct reason for the dearth of

traditional African-American Christmas music. However, in *Ev'ry Time I Feel the Spirit*, Gwendolin Sims Warren offers an even more practical explanation: " . . . the Bible itself speaks more of the death and resurrection of Jesus than it does of His birth."

Even in the gospel songs and spirituals devoted to celebrating Jesus' birth, a considerable number of the lines and verses instead recount how He suffered and died on the cross. Clearly, our ancestors could identify with the lowly birth of the infant Jesus amidst the straw and animals, yet they were more fully drawn to Jesus the Man who, after suffering so greatly for sins not of His own making, was able to escape even from death. Having so many crosses of their own to bear, our people have needed throughout the years an image of a Savior who could share our burdens and lighten our loads, both literally and

figuratively. At the risk of sounding a bit too facetious, images of the Infant Jesus lying in swaddling clothes in a manger must have seemed to some of our ancestors too much like someone they would have to take care of—and not enough like someone who could take care of them!

FOLLOWING THAT STAR

I t is ironic and unfortunate that sometimes these old spirituals have been, even by our own people, lumped together and dismissed derisively as slave songs. These so-called slave songs were actually one of the tools our ancestors used to escape slavery. Sometimes this escape was only psychological. However, in the lives of an oppressed people, opportunities for psychological escape may be just as rare and critical as opportunities for physical escape. Some have suggested, in an over-simplification, that Christianity encouraged slaves to settle for heaven later rather than to fight for freedom in the present. We know, however, from

the songs that have been passed down to us through the generations, that our ancestors had their own ideas about what it meant to be a Christian. As one of our most beloved spirituals points out, "Everybody talking about heaven ain't going there." Our ancestors saw the irony in the fact that so-called followers of Christ were holding them in bondage.

Both as a safety measure and as a strategic measure, our forebears made a point of seeming to practice an acceptable form of Christianity. Meanwhile, within their hearts and within their songs, our people were secretly preparing to help make real the promises of the prophet Isaiah:

Hast though not known? Hast thou not heard that *the everlasting God, the LORD, the Creator of the ends of the earth, fainteth not, neither is weary?* there is *no searching of his understanding. He*

giveth power to the faint; and to them that have *no might he increaseth strength. . . . but they that wait upon the LORD shall renew* their *strength; they shall mount up with wings as eagles; they shall run, and not be weary;* and *they shall walk, and not faint*

Isaiah 40:28-29, 31 (KJV).

Again and again in African-American spirituals and gospel songs, listeners are admonished to "follow the star." These star songs have had many different meanings throughout our history as a people. Songs such as "Rise Up, Shepherd, and Follow" and "Behold That Star" were just as likely to be used to map the way to freedom in the North as they were to praise the birth of Jesus. The story of the wise men following the Star of Bethlehem took on special meaning for slaves seeking to get to freedom via

the Underground Railroad. Just as the shepherds and wise men depended on a star in the East to guide them on their way to see the new Savior, our ancestors depended on the North Star and the Big Dipper to light their way to freedom and better opportunities. Just as spirituals often contained secret directions to freedom for slaves, they also were the songs that gave strength to the freedom fighters of the Civil Rights Movement. The Christian faith that the slaves came to know is the same faith that would eventually launch their great-grandchildren's struggle for freedom in the Civil Rights Movement. This faith gives assurance that indeed a Savior has been born to bring liberty to the oppressed.

CHILDREN OF THE JUBILEE

Gospel music is "jubilee" music. Although a jubilee is, indeed, a joyful celebration, it is also much more than that. In the twenty-fifth chapter of the Book of Leviticus it is proclaimed that every fiftieth year should be a year of jubilee. Passages from Leviticus 25 explain jubilee as follows:

> And the sabbath of the land shall be meat for you; for thee, and for
> thy servant, and for thy maid, and for thy hired servant, and for
> thy stranger that sojourneth with thee . . .
>
> *Leviticus 25:6 (KJV)*

And ye shall hallow the fiftieth year, and proclaim liberty through-out all *the land unto all the inhabitants thereof: it shall be a jubilee unto you; and ye shall return every man unto his family.*

Leviticus 25:10 (KJV)

Ye shall not therefore oppress one another; but thou shalt fear thy God: for I am *the LORD your God.*

Leviticus 25:17 (KJV)

During the time of jubilee, all debts were to be forgiven and all slaves restored to freedom. In *Lyrics of the Afro-American Spiritual: A Documentary Collection*, it is written that the word "jubal" is an original Hebrew root word meaning "principle of sound; source of joy; source of moral affections; source of happiness; cry of joy;

jubilation; a constant stream; moral prosperity; harmony; melody; music." Jubal is the father of the harp and pipe and the spiritual father of all who inspire worship and awe through music.

After reading the book of Leviticus, we are not surprised that our African ancestors were able to embrace the Scriptures so wholeheartedly. They could identify with the stories of the enslaved Hebrews. Spirituals like "Didn't My Lord Deliver Daniel (then why not every man?)" provide examples of how our ancestors made the heroes of the Hebrews into their own champions. Like the ancient Hebrews, our people too felt the connections between joy and righteousness, liberty and song. It was only natural to the ancient Hebrews and to the Africans who found themselves in America to use music to keep alive in their souls the sense of justice they were prevented from experiencing in their daily lives.

The Jewish concept of jubilee took a strong hold on the

African-American cultural imagination and it is retained to this day. Evidence of the significance of jubilee in contemporary gospel music can be found anywhere one cares to look. How many African-American churches in a given year go without hosting at least one Gospel Jubilee Picnic or having in their midst at least one Gospel Jubilee choir?

The lives of our African-American ancestors were filled with daily anguish and humiliation, but through their faith and with their music they were able to keep alive a sense of majesty. They believed in the promise of eventual triumph over adversity. This sense of promise is as evident in the spirituals that arose out of our days in the cotton fields as it is in the gospel music we created as we struggled later for survival as free people in the cities. The songs of our people which honor the birth of Jesus—even the songs created in our bleakest moments—never fail to mention a sense of impending victory over hardship and suffering.

GETTIN' HAPPY WITH THE SPIRIT

Like some brilliant form of spiritual alchemy, gospel music takes the dross from the problems that weigh our spirits down and transforms it into a shinier and more precious metal. As weary believers we drag ourselves into church on Sunday carrying the weight of the week on our shoulders. Not expecting much more of our day than just to get through it, we are surprised to find ourselves "feelin' the Spirit" before the choir has even made it through the first chorus of "Lord Will Make a Way Somehow." We can tell our outlook is changing for the better during "We'll Understand It Better By and By." By the time

the congregation and choir join together in singing "My God Is Real (Yes, God Is Real)" we are for sure "gettin' happy," as the old folks used to say. Then, as the services draw to a close to the soothing strains of "There's a Sweet, Sweet Spirit (In This Place)," we wonder what ever led us to think we were losing our strength in the first place. For the rest of the week, just the memory of Deacon Jones standing up and singing "Stand By Me" during altar call is enough to make us smile to ourselves.

Gospel songs remind us that our people have always been able to find joy in life. Even when we have been given no reasons for joy from without, we have always managed to find reasons within. Considering the sorrow out of which it is so often born, gospel music is doubly amazing because it always carries with it such an innate sense of jubilation. Thomas Dorsey composed "Precious Lord, Take My Hand" after losing his wife and baby

to the complications of childbirth. Even the standard Protestant hymns which appeal to the gospel ear tend to be odes to the phoenix-like faith that can arise from the ashes of our lives' tragedies. By time he was 25, the Irishman Joseph Scriven, who penned the gospel favorite, "What A Friend We Have In Jesus," had already lost two fiancées to death, suffered a chronic illness, lost a promising career in the military, and lived and worked among the destitute. He lost his life at that age by drowning, but he never lost his faith.

Every week, gospel choirs lead congregations back to hope through singing Scriven's words: "Have we trials and temptations? Is there trouble anywhere? We should never be discouraged. Take it to the Lord in prayer."

Perhaps the secret of gospel music is that at the very least gospel's heights of joy are equal to the depths of life's despairs.

Gospel music is about having faith in the future in spite of the bleakness of the past or the uncertainty of the present. Gospel's faith is not the faith of the innocent who are only faithful because they have not yet been tried. Gospel's faith is one that says in the words of African-American folk wisdom: "He knows just how much we can bear." We maintain a sense of hope from knowing that God never abandons the faithful or leaves us without help. We believe that salvation will surely come even if we are not sure where or when. Another African-American folk saying reminds us, "God may not come when you want Him to, but He is always right on time." We have learned to walk steadily through life's dangers by "Leaning on the Everlasting Arms."

In these difficult times, as our communities stagger under the burdens of violence, drug abuse, unemployment, teen

pregnancy, and family breakdown, we need gospel's sense of peace in the face of adversity as least as much as we ever have before. Gospel music is a reminder that those who came before us were able to keep on "Marching towards Zion" even as they struggled against the inhumanity of slavery, the devastation of the Great Depression, or the indignity of segregation. If our ancestors could find reasons to keep believing in a better life as they watched their children being sold and the fruits of their labor unjustly taken away, then surely we as a free people can somehow maintain the strength and conviction we need to fly above the obstacles blocking our path.

BEARING THE GOOD TIDINGS

Although there are not many gospel songs whose lyrics are explicitly devoted to Christmas, there is a larger sense in which *all* gospel songs are Christmas songs. Christmas is the "good news" holiday and gospel is music devoted to spreading the good news.

Whether we are singing a gospel song for all occasions like "This Little Light of Mine" or a seasonal gospel selection such as "Glory To Dat Newborn King," the lyrics remind us to release ourselves from the chains of fear, knowing that One has come to help us transcend our sorrows. In fact, the titles of so many gospel songs and spirituals read like news bulletins and instruct us to make sure this message gets passed around: "You Kin Tell De World Bout Dis!" "Good News!" "Great Day, Great Day!" "Mizz Mary Had a Baby!" "Rise Up Shepherds and Follow!" "Glory, Glory Hallelujah!" "Go Tell It On The Mountain!"

Gospel music, despite the assertions of its early nay-sayers, has always been true to its name. In the Bible, the Gospels are the first four books of the New Testament. These books—Matthew, Mark, Luke, and John—tell the story of Jesus Christ, the son of God, who was sent as a Savior to restore all of God's children to Grace. The four Apostles were disciples of Christ who devoted the rest of their lives to teaching others what Jesus taught them. In the Book of John we find what is perhaps the single most quoted verse in all the New Testament. Some Christians believe in the power of these words so strongly that they often invoke just the phrase—"John Three-Sixteen"—as a blessing:

For God so loved the world, that he gave his only begotten Son, that whosoever believeth in him should not perish, but have ever-lasting life. For God sent not his Son into the world to condemn the world; but that the world through him might be saved.

John 3:16-17 (KJV)

The word "gospel" literally means "good news." Following in the footsteps of Jesus' disciples, gospel music has always existed for only one purpose: to spread the good news of God's enduring love for humanity.

Now that you know, friend, "go tell it on the mountain!"